Surviving Anything with

God

by Your Side

Surviving Anything with

God

by Your Side

ASWANA ANGELS

iUniverse, Inc.
Bloomington

Surviving Anything with God by Your Side

iUniverse books may be ordered through booksellers or by contacting:

iUniverse
1663 Liberty Drive
Bloomington, IN 47403
www.iuniverse.com
1-800-Authors (1-800-288-4677)

Because of the dynamic nature of the Internet, any web addresses or links contained in this book may have changed since publication and may no longer be valid. The views expressed in this work are solely those of the author and do not necessarily reflect the views of the publisher, and the publisher hereby disclaims any responsibility for them.

Any people depicted in stock imagery provided by Thinkstock are models, and such images are being used for illustrative purposes only.
Certain stock imagery © Thinkstock.

ISBN: 978-1-4759-8566-5 (sc)
ISBN: 978-1-4759-8567-2 (ebk)

Printed in the United States of America

iUniverse rev. date: 04/29/2013

DEDICATION

I would like to dedicate this book to Fran DeSeno, a Reike Master.

She not only healed me through her expertise in Reike at her place of business but also she can perform long distance Reike and has performed it on me with amazing results! She also gave me back the most important thing in my life! She taught me how to get back in touch with God even though I always believed in God, because of all the hurt I went through, I shut him out of my life without my even knowing that I did.

She taught me the steps that I needed to get back in touch with God and the Universe, she has also taught me so many other things, I am truly grateful that she came into my life when I needed it most and I am so blessed from the bottom of my heart and soul for everything she has done in the past and still does for me continuously.

We have become friends through all of this, which is the next greatest joy, of course, the first greatest joy was to remove the blockage that I did to myself blocking God out of my life and asking him to return into my life. He never left me, I left him, unknowingly.

Since then my life has taken a complete 360 degree turn around. Sure, I have challenges just like probably everyone else, but Fran taught me how to release them to God and he will take care of them and do what is best.

I am so grateful to Fran, for without her coming into my life, and with her kindness, generosity and help who knows where my life would be at this moment.

She not only helped me but she helps anyone that she can, sometimes the only way she can do this is by long distance.

I LOVE HER WITH ALL MY HEART AND SOUL and would just like to say THANK YOU FOR EVERYTHING YOU HAVE DONE FOR ME AND CONTINUES TO DO!!!

SHE IS DEFINITELY, IN MY OPINION AN EARTH ANGEL, AS WELL AS OTHERS, SHE IS HERE TO HELP THOSE THAT NEED HELP!!!

I WOULD LIKE TO THANK GOD FOR BEING SO PATIENT AND WELCOMING ME BACK TO HIM WITH OPEN ARMS, AND BEING ABLE TO COMMUNICATE WITH HIM IN A MUCH STRONGER, MORE PASSIONATE WAY THAN I COULD HAVE EVER IMAGINED.

WITHOUT HIM AND ALL HIS HELPERS, TO NAME A FEW THE ANGELS, ASCENDED MASTERS, ARCHANGELS, AND THE LIST GOES ON, I CAN HONESTLY SAY I WOULD NOT BE WHERE I AM TODAY!

Sure, I still have challenges as does everyone, but when you have the faith and really deep down in your heart you know that your prayers are being heard and are going to be answered, it is such a GREAT FEELING.

The outcome of what you prayed about might be something totally different than what you thought it was going to be, but you must remember God knows what is best for you, even though at the moment that it happens you don't understand, in his Diving Timing, you will understand exactly why things happened to you and why.

TABLE OF CONTENTS

PREFACE

I believe in God to pray, but you can go to your higher power, it is all the same and works the same way.

The fact remains that you have to open your heart and mind, pray and have the faith, even though your patience will be tested; it will come to you, when the timing is right.

In my book, I'm referring to God, and his helpers because that is my belief; but by all means I'm not being prejudice, this is only an easy, understandable guide to help you, the way it has helped me. I also want you to pray in whomever you believe in, as I know that there are numerous religions in the world in this present day, pray to the one you believe in.

If you think that it won't work for you, just because it worked for me, well all I can say to you is, you will never know—unless you try. You will be amazed as to what happens not only to yourself, but how it affects the people around you, whether they are loved ones or even a stranger.

This is not a very complicated system you have to do, there are just certain things you have to do and/or possibly change the way you are doing them or thinking about something, which are very easy to learn, to make your life a better one than which you are living in now.

I will give you a few examples in each chapter as to what happened to me and the outcome which will totally amaze you!

GOD WORKS IN MYSTERIOUS WAYS BUT ALWAYS IN THE BEST INTEREST AND FOR THE BENEFIT OF EVERYONE INVOLVED!!! IT IS A GREAT BLESSING TO ALL MANKIND THAT HE IS ALWAYS FORGIVING AND CONTINOUSLY TRYING TO MAKE OUR LIVES BETTER; A LIFE OF HAPPINESS, JOY AND PEACE.

GRANTED THERE WILL BE CHALLENGES IN EVERYONES' LIFE, BUT THESE WERE MEANT TO TEACH US LESSONS TO HELP OUR SOUL GROW, DURING A LIFETIME. YOU WILL FIND IF YOU LOOK BACK AND THINK ABOUT A CHALLENGE YOU FACED AND THE LESSON THAT YOU LEARNT AND HOW YOU BECAME A BETTER AND STRONGER PERSON. IF YOU DIDN'T LEARN ANYTHING THING ABOUT THE CHALLENGE, IT WILL DEFINITELY BE REPEATED AGAIN AND AGAIN TO YOU UNTIL YOU FINALLY LEARNT THE LESSON; YOU HAVE GOD TO THANK FOR THAT!

CHAPTER ONE

Stop Being The Victim—Know Your Good Qualities And Feel And Believe In Yourself

When something happens in our lives, most of the time we let our egos' take over our normal thinking, making us think that we are the victim of the times or the situation we are in.

This can be overcome by a very simple step, although you must believe, have faith and realize all the good qualities that you as an individual have inside yourself.

Just think of the type of person that you are, for example, kind, loving, caring, generous, honest, trustworthy; these are just a few examples, you can add as many or as few as you want. The more you add to your list about yourself, the more you will realize that you are really not a victim at all.

Keep repeating this list to yourself at least once a day, when you won't be interrupted and you will find yourself adding more and more about yourself to this list as you start to really realize the person who you really are.

If you got laid off, and thought that you were the victim; you will soon realize that it was just circumstances of the times we are in.

If you are in a relationship where you are always the giver and not getting back what you deserve, this is when you will realize it. Once you know your qualities, everything else falls in place. It's amazing, but true. Now will be the time when you have to choose whether you want to remain in this relationship and whether there is any hope of your partner realizing your needs and if he or she is willing to change, or if things are going to continue going the way they are now. I am not telling you to leave a relationship, only you can make that decision, despite how hard it might be, you must think of your needs.

If your needs are not met and you continuously hold them inside of you, the only thing that happens is that another part of your body, will take on what you are feeling and the possibilities of an illness could be inevitable, not always, but the possibility is there.

You might try counseling to see if that helps change the situation you are in, hopefully it does and continues to be good; but you must remember to let your partner know what you need. If everything turns out for the best, Congratulations!!! Just don't forget to thank God for intervening on both of you to have this relationship work, as he knows best.

Why the decision for you might be so hard to make is because even though the situation you are in is not what you want, you somehow hope and pray that your partner will change or you somehow accepted that this was how it is going to be. For you to leave an unhealthy situation is not an easy decision at all, you are going out on your own and having to support yourself and your children or pets if you have them. This is not easy, especially if you are not making much money or you haven't been working; or you are hesitant about this type of change, especially in the world's situation today.

Most of us don't like change; we just go with the flow and hope that things get better. Usually they stay the same, sometimes they do change but that is not the normal situation, or they change for a while and then the pattern repeats itself.

This is when you must think of yourself for a change and ask yourself, "Is this really how I want it to be for the rest of my life?"

You will find that the answer will pop in your head rather quickly.

Once you have made your decision as to what you plan to do, take action even if it is small steps at a time. Don't forget to pray to God for help and guidance during this transition period; he will gladly help you through everything. Make sure that you cover and ask as many questions to professionals that can help you to make a sound decision.

Whether it is going to counseling again and hope that it helps like it did before, or you both go separate ways, definitely check and double check everything; now that you made your decision, your must think of each step, no matter how small, to get to where you want to be and how you are going to make this accomplishment a success. Pray to God for help in making the decision and to give you guidance and help you to decide which is best for you. God knows what is best for all of us, all we have to do, is ASK!

If your decision is to leave, you will probably have challenges in your life, despite all the preparation you did prior to your leaving. Don't become scared or worried, this is just God's way of helping to learn lessons in our lives, which we need to learn in life, in order for us to grow. Again, pray to God for help and to take these scared and worried feelings away from you and replace them with calm, peaceful, loving, positive and faithful feelings and also ask him to help you get through. Once you pray, even though the challenge might still be there until you learn the lesson that was meant to be learnt, you will find that somehow you being scared and worried are not there, you will know deep in your heart; and also have a sense telling you that somehow, someway everything will turn out fine.

CHAPTER TWO

LISTEN TO YOUR INNER VOICE

All of us have what is called an inner voice. It is something in our head we hear telling us to do or not to do something. Normally, we would take this as our own thoughts and sometimes they might be; however, when there is a distinct voice telling you to either do something or not do something, then that is definitely your Guardian Angel or another angel guiding you for your best interest, but you must remember that you would have to pray and ask them for guidance.

When one prays to God or whomever they believe in, you might ask for help, and at this point this is where you are allowing the angels to intervene and help you, without your asking, the only time they are allowed to intervene is when something is going to happen to you and you would die before your time.

You have to be willing to accept this and when one has faith, this is an automatic happening. You might try to fight and think that it is just your ego or a thought you have; but when the little voice continues and if you ignore it, it just becomes louder and louder, then you know that it is one of God's helpers talking and guiding you.

Fran came into my life at this time and taught me how to open up to God even more so than I did before, which was DEFINITELY SOMETHING I WILL CHERISH FOR THE REST OF MY LIFE—and good things started happening to me, thanks to God and his angels and the rest of his helpers. Here are a few examples:

THE MOST IMPORTANT THING THAT HAPPENED AS FAR AS LISTENING TO MY INNER VOICE; IS THIS BOOK!!!

I kept hearing "WRITE", but I let it go, I didn't have time to write and I didn't even know what to write about.

I kept hearing almost every morning and even during the day "WRITE", so finally one morning, I answered and said, "Write what?" I heard back, "A BOOK".

My reply was, "About what and what should the title be?" Then the most miraculous thing happened, I heard the name of this book! I thanked God, but let it go. God didn't, the following day; I heard the same thing, as before, "WRITE, I GAVE YOU THE TITLE". I said, "Yes, you did, but what about the Chapters and what do I say, will you help me?" Then all of a sudden I heard all the chapters in the book, giving me time to write them down.

I asked if they would help me to write this book, as I have no idea where or how to go about it. The reply was, "We will take care of everything; the book needs to get out into the public immediately!"

I then said to God, "Yes, I will write it for you, as long as you are telling me what to write." Believe it or not, but that is exactly what is happening! AMAZING, COINCIDENCE, NEITHER ONE—IT IS A MIRACLE IN PROGRESS!!!

One beautiful morning during the winter, the sun was shining and the weather was really unusually warm, it was probably around 50 degrees at 7:30 am, which in the Northeast is not common. I was getting ready for work and putting on my jeans, as the job I had at that time allowed me to wear jeans and I was more comfortable with jeans on anyway, so that's why I had my jeans on. I did my normal routine before going to work, and as I was doing this after I got dressed, I heard a little voice saying to me, "Go shave your legs." So the first time I heard it, I shrugged it off. It kept repeating itself to me and I spoke out and said "I have jeans on, nobody will see my legs; I will shave my legs when I get home." I didn't want to be late to work. The little voice inside my head was getting louder and louder, and even more demanding, "SHAVE YOUR LEGS NOW!"

I tried to ignore the voice getting louder and louder and went to go out the door and I COULDN'T OPEN

THE DOOR! THEN THE VOICE, IN KIND OF A DEMANDING BUT LOVING WAY AGAIN SAID, "SHAVE YOUR LEGS NOW!!!"

I couldn't understand why the door wouldn't open, so I glanced at the clock and figured I could go and shave my legs quick and still be into work on time, so I said to this voice, "O.K. YOU WIN—I'M GOING TO GO SHAVE MY LEGS, I DON'T KNOW WHY, BUT I'LL DO IT!"

While I was shaving my legs, the telephone rang and it was my boss on the other end. I was surprised hearing from him and he said to me, "Have you looked outside?" I didn't want to tell him about the little voice, he probably would have thought I was nuts, so I just said, "No, I was just getting ready and I'm about to leave now."

He said, "Look outside!" I looked outside and we had a hail storm go through and the roads were completely covered in ice. This was a freak storm that passed through, the sun wasn't out anymore and it was hailing hard. I said to my boss, "When did this start?" He replied, "Just a few minutes ago, and came so fast, it shocked everybody, and people are sliding everywhere as they don't have any control of their cars and there are accidents everywhere. That's why I called you before you left because you are safe at home and don't come in until the roads are clear." I thanked him and hung up.

I said, "THANK YOU ANGELS!!!" I finally understood why this little voice was so persistent and saved my life.

I would have been right in the middle of this freak hail storm that came in a split second with my car, which was a 1989 Firebird with the wide tires. I definitely would have been in trouble.

The angels helped save my life by being so persistent even to the point of not letting me out of my own door. When the roads were clear to go to work, the door opened just as it always had before, I smiled to myself and said, Thank you again for saving my life."

Here is another example of how my inner voice helped me:

After that I would always listen to my inner voice and would never question what they were telling me to do, except one other time. It was 6:00 am and I stopped in the supermarket to pick up a few things before going into work early this one particular day. There was one cashier and she had a couple customers. I kept hearing go back to Isle 5 but I kept ignoring it. I picked up the couple things which I needed and as I was heading to the register to get checked out I heard my inner voice again, go back to Isle 5. This time I listened before checking out and went to see what was in Isle 5 that was so important.

I've been in this supermarket many times but had no idea what was in Isle 5. When I got to the Isle being in a rush and glanced to my left and it was the spot where all the cards for all occasions were displayed. I thought to myself, I don't need a card. Then I heard my inner voice say, "Look to the right" I looked and saw candles. I said to my inner voice, "I'm afraid to light candles", (When I was 10 years old, I decided to make a candle out of crayons. I got an empty can and put the crayons in the can, put them on the stove and watched them melt, all of a sudden—the can caught on fire. Not knowing what to do I added water and the flame mushroomed. I was so afraid the house was going to burn down but thankfully someone came into the house at the same time and took care of the situation. Needless to say, I definitely got in trouble for trying something so stupid without supervision of an adult but I will never forget that feeling. Well that episode scared me so much, that I never lit a candle after that). The voice insisted to pick up a candle, and I continued to argue that I was afraid of them. Then my inner voice said to me in a demanding but loving way, "Matter of fact, pick up two candles right now!" It was a good thing nobody was around listening to me talk to myself, they would have thought I was crazy. So I listened, didn't look at the name of them and rushed back to the register. I put each candle in a separate bag and then put them both in the same bag, I then bagged my other things I picked up and took the bags. I paid the cashier, said, "Thanks and have a good day!" and went to work.

When I came home after work, I brought in the house the few things I bought, including the candles. I left the bag with the candles in it, in the kitchen on the floor and never took them out. When I went downstairs, as this is where I made it my sacred place, I heard the little voice again, "Where are the candles?" I said, "Upstairs." Then the voice said, "Well go get them." I tried ignoring my little voice again, but they would not give up, the voice kept getting louder and louder, so I finally said, "O.K., I'll go get them." I came upstairs and brought them downstairs and just set them on the floor next to me. The little voice in my head again spoke and said, "Well, take one out and light it." I said, "No, I told you I was afraid of candles!" The voice in a very loving way told me, "Take the candle out and light it, everything will be fine, you will see!" So I listened and took the candle out and lit it. It was amazing, I became so calm and relaxed with such a peacefulness all around me, I left it burning until I was ready to come back upstairs. I said, "Thank You for having me buy the candles, I feel so good!"

Please remember not to light candles around children or pets because a child could get burnt very easily, or if a pet walked by the lit candle their fur could catch on fire. Bring your candle to a special place where you are by yourself.

After that I always listen to my inner voice and never question it at all, and everything always works out sometimes even better than I could have imagined.

CHAPTER THREE

How To Handle Challenges

Everyday of our lives we all go through some kind of a challenge. There is a reason for these challenges whether they are noticed or not.

Challenges are sent to us from above to learn a lesson, if we don't learn it the first time, it will repeat itself until we finally learn it, and only then will that challenge cease to exist.

It seems that with the busy life that we are living in these times that, so many of the small challenges we just take them with a grain of salt and keep going with our normal lifestyle.

The only time that we notice a challenge is when it starts to become an insurmountable amount of challenge which is far to much for us to ignore and that's when we stop and realize, "What do we do next?"

Usually, the first step is panic and/or anxiety sets in, then we try to dismiss it figuring that it will go away if we forget about it. Actually what happens, is that this challenge keeps getting bigger and bigger.

The next step is worrying about what we are going to do in order to rectify this challenge. We start thinking of all of our options and try to make a choice. When we find out the choice that we made is not working and the challenge is still there, we find other ways in which to change our ways of living.

We find out after changing many things in our lifestyle, that nothing is working and we are constantly thinking about the challenge which lies ahead for us, being that of loosing a job and where can we find another one to make ends meet, or loosing our home and what can we do in order to keep it, the list goes on and on.

The common denominator in this total amount of challenge is that our ways of thinking are not changing. Yes physically we are changing our lifestyle to compensate, when actually what needs to be changed is our way of thinking.

Have faith in God, or whomever you believe in, pray and ask for help. Trust that your prayers will be answered in a way probably not the way you think that they should be, but what God or whomever you are praying to, knows what is best for us. We must take the leap of faith, trust it and stay positive despite what we look at as the reality of the situation we are in.

Deep down inside, we must keep the faith at all times, and stay positive knowing that everything will turn out the way that God knows is best for us.

Also one cannot forget what you think is what you are attracting into your life! This is so important to understand. There are many books that explain this concept. They even have cards for you, so that you may shuffle them, pray for guidance and then listen to your inner voice and pick out the cards you are told to pick out. This will let you know what you are attracting into your life. I will talk more about in Chapter 6.

For instance, if you are thinking that you are poor and don't have any money, that is exactly what the Universe is going to send to you, there is no other way that it works. What you think is exactly what you will receive back.

I understand that it is very hard to think that you have more than enough money, when you only have $1.00 in your wallet, but you have to think, feel and know that you will have hundreds of dollars in your wallet and in the bank, picture it in your mind, have the faith that it will happen and the Universe will deliver to you. Our thoughts are not manifested immediately; there is a buffer of time, just in case you change your mind on something. Our thoughts might be manifested in a totally different way than what we expect, but again you must remember the Universe knows which is best for us, despite what we might think.

With our faith and positive thinking you will find that when the timing is right, everything will fall into place and you will also probably find that it is even more and even better than what you asked for in the first place.

The hardest part of this process is to keep the faith regardless of what is thrown into your path, and to keep a positive attitude with the knowingness that everything will work out in God's Divine Timing. We must also have the patience to wait for the Divine Timing when this will occur, as we have no control over that at all.

Personally, I have been challenged many times, especially these past 5 years, it wasn't until I started praying, listening and opening my mind to God and the angels who were trying to talk with me, but I previously shut them out.

I finally opened myself up, which I will explain how to do in the next chapter, and I started listening, surrendered my challenges to God along with the anxiety, fear and all the rest of the negative feelings I had. This is when I finally saw little by little my life starting to change. I also prayed to the angels, asking them to help me (as much as they would like to intervene to help us-they are not allowed to-unless it's life or death before our time) to change my thoughts back to positive, if I slip back into thinking negative.

They did that with pleasure for me and I now find myself thinking positive all the time. I take a negative situation and turn it into a positive one within a very short time. I thank them every time that it happens,

I'm only human to let negative thoughts come into my mind, however; as time goes by, I find that there are less and less negative thoughts coming to me. When I am in a negative situation, like my boss letting me go, the first thought that comes to mind is "Well this is not the job that was meant for me to be in, there is another purpose in life that I am suppose to follow and this job was not bringing me closer to the path on which I am suppose to take."

I am not by any means trying to minimize the hurt of loosing a job and a paycheck, but what I am trying to have you understand is—there is a reason for everything that happens to not only you, but everyone.

In one of the books I had bought to learn how to communicate with animals, there was a section that had different animals, insects, etc. and what the meaning of seeing them was.

Well one day while I was driving I saw 6 hawks. Seeing a hawk means that a messenger from the skies are telling you to be prepared for challenge but a wise interception is going to intervene and keep you on your sacred path.

Seeing these 6 hawks, all the same day, I have to admit even though I had total faith in God, I was scared. All I kept thinking of 6 challenges all at the same time, how can I do it myself? Then I heard the inner voice, "Pray"

I went and lit the candle and started crying as hard if not harder than when I lost one of my cats and started praying to God. I remember as if it were today, I said,"

God, I can't handle 6 challenges all at the same time, what are you trying to do to me?" I am crying so hard, the tears were just streaming down my face, and I could feel my stomach hurting from crying so hard, when ALL OF A SUDDEN I HEARD: "You only get what you can handle my child." I then replied, "But all 6 at once, I can't do it? I need your help, please help me?" I again heard the reply, "You only get what you can handle my child, you will be fine, my child." I IMMEDIATELY STOPPED CRYING AND THERE WAS SUCH A PEACEFUL, CALM FEELING INSIDE OF ME, AND I COULD SENSE THAT GOD AND ALL HIS HELPERS WERE ALL AROUND ME!!! I THANKED GOD, BLEW OUT THE CANDLE. I HAD TO LOOK AT THE NAME OF THE CANDLE AS I NEVER DID BEFORE—BELIEVE IT OR NOT—THE NAME WAS ANGEL KISSES. I SMILED TO MYSELF AND THANKED THE ANGELS AND WENT TO BED.

The next day, I did receive all 6 challenges, one right after the other. I wasn't afraid because of the message I received the night before and everything went exactly how God said it would, I handle every single one of them and felt very peaceful and calm while doing it. I also felt God and all his helpers around me to succeed in tackling each challenge.

Ever since then, when I saw a hawk I wasn't frightened any longer, cause I knew that from the lesson which I was so fortunate that God taught me and I learnt my lesson, that everything would turn out fine.

CHAPTER FOUR

How To Relax And Talk With God Or Whomever You Believe In

The most important thing is to find a place where you can go and not be interrupted by anything at all. If you are doing this in your home, make sure the telephone is turned off so that you don't hear the ring, turn off the television and/or radio. You must have complete silence for as long as you need.

Now that you found the area that you are not going to be disturbed, you must find a very comfortable place for you to sit and also have a table in front of you, it does not have to be large, but it does have to be sturdy as you will be placing a candle on it.

When picking out a candle to perform this relaxation and process you can do two things, you can ask the angels to help you pick out the candle you need, and trust me on this, they will certainly pick the one that you personally need, or you can pick one that has a very calm, peaceful scent when you smell it.

Start by lighting the candle and then start to deep breath and concentrating on your breathing and let everything in your mind go blank, just keep concentrating on your breathing. As you are doing this, look at the candle, which you lit, at first, you might not see anything except the flame of the candle which is fine. This procedure might have to be done more than once before you start to see things happening, which is very normal; the important thing is that you stay relaxed during this process. If nothing happens after doing this for a while, don't get discouraged; just try it again either later if you have a chance or the following day.

Eventually, you will notice as you are relaxing and looking into the flame of the candle you'll start to see different colors appear even though your eyes are wide open. Don't be alarmed by this, all this means is that you are finally learning how to relax and be able to talk with God and hear what he is telling you.

The more you practice this process, the easier it is to hear God's message to you. You can also communicate with him in this manner, if you have a question or questions, just ask him and as you sit there looking into the candle you will hear his voice coming through to you. It will always be a very loving message and positive.

When I first did this, I saw different colors finally, as it took me a while. The first color that I saw was a black circle, that sacred me, not knowing what it was or what it meant. I stuck with it and eventually the black circle had a red dot in it, then two red dots apart from one another and then joining together as one, and then I started to see different colors coming in such as green, blue, violet, white, etc.

This is very normal and nothing to be afraid of, you will find that the more relaxed you are, the colors will come to you at a faster pace than if you are tense. The colors that you see are nothing to be afraid of at all, it is a part of you and you trying to connect with God.

When I want to talk with God, I just light my candle, look at the flame, become relaxed and ask the question and patiently wait for the answer.

In the beginning, don't think that if you don't hear anything you are doing something wrong, just have the patience and keep trying. There is one thing that will try to interfere with what God is telling you and what your ego is telling you.

That's what happened to me, but then I told my ego get out of the way, I want to hear God and not you. Your ego always has some negativity in it, and that is how you can recognize it. Once saying it to my ego was enough, it never interfered with my speaking with God.

When doing this exercise you will always hear something that God has to tell you, but it is always in a loving, calming, peaceful way. God might also have what I would call a nickname. As for me, when God talks with me at the end of what he wants to tell me, he always ends it with the "My Child."

The only thing I can tell you is that you will definitely know that the message was directly from God talking with you just by then ending. Once you hear the ending of your conversation from God it never varies, it is always the same. At least that is how it is for me. If I hear another message without the ending that God uses then I know and am able to sense if it is from an angel, archangel or one of God's others helpers.

You might hear the same words which is fine or something entirely different, but it will always be the same.

After you have received the answer to your questions that you asked and you are through for this session, always remember to Thank God for talking with you and that you appreciate him taking his time to re-assure you and giving you an answer.

You will find that after talking with God, you will be very calm, peaceful and have such a wonderful, warm feeling is all around you.

There is no special time, nor how many times during the day or night that you would like to do this; you may do it as many times as you like. All you have to remember is God is always there waiting for you and never to busy to hear your prayers.

You will receive no matter what you ask; you will always receive an answer. It might not be the one that you wanted to hear, but God knows what is best for us, even if we can't understand why he said that. It might be that there is another lesson which we have to learn in life; and that is the reason. You will understand when the timing is right, sometimes it might not be immediately or even a day.

It was then, that I realized the POWER OF PRAYER and how God watches over all of us, for our best interest, even though the outcome might not be at all what we expect, but never question the outcome.

CHAPTER FIVE

LEARN HOW TO GO INSIDE YOURSELF AND GET TO KNOW EXACTLY WHO YOU ARE AND WHAT YOU REALLY AND WHAT YOU WANT TO DO WITH YOUR LIFE

One really needs to find out who they really are inside, not who they have become due to outside influences in our lives; but really your own true self. You will be amazed when doing this, what you really find out about yourself.

Again, you need to go to your quiet place, light the candle and relax. This might take a while, especially if you had a very tense day, and you haven't had a chance to unwind. Take your time and don't rush this process.

Once you finally become relaxed and empty your mind of everything, start looking at the candle and let your mind stay empty.

Start noticing your breathing, how you are inhaling and exhaling. Concentrate on this for a while, and you will find that you are even more relaxed than you were before.

Now, start slowly and concentrate on your heart. Don't try to think anything, just remain quiet and concentrate on your heart, and continue your breathing and the aroma of the candle you lit.

You will start to notice different feelings that are coming to you, and also thoughts that are coming into your mind. This is your heart and soul talking with you, telling you how they are feeling and what it wants. It is now up to you, whether you want to be true to yourself and your heart's desires, or continue to go the way you have always done previously.

Don't be alarmed if you start to cry, this might happen, as it did to me.

I was always so use to giving of myself to others; that I never once gave it a thought as to how I really felt. My main concern was to make others happy and to do whatever I could to make that happen.

By my looking inside my heart and listening to what it was telling me, I was depriving myself of the love which I deserved and also being used and taken for granted; never receiving anything in return. My heart was breaking from my actions of always putting myself last. I started sobbing uncontrollably and then I prayed to God for help, which he gladly gave me, but I knew that I had to listen to my heart and what my heart was telling me, no matter how much it hurt me to hear it.

I again went back into my heart and asked my heart what if anything I should do so that it would stop hurting; it was then that I heard CHANGE THE WAY YOU ARE DOING THINGS! It was then that I realized that I didn't have to stop giving because I enjoyed making others happy, but do it to the ones who appreciated it.

My heart also told me what my true desires were, and how to make each desire happen.

Before leaving my heart, I thanked my heart for talking with me and letting me know exactly how it was feeling and what I should do.

I then went to other parts of my body and if there was a message from a particular organ then I would hear something in my mind, otherwise it would be silent.

To this day, I still do this every once in a while, to make sure that my heart is happy and my true desires are still the same or if there are more desires in which my heart added to become a fulfilled individual.

I do find my heart desiring to accomplish more in life, with helping others, but it has also expanded to helping animals, wildlife, nature and the environment.

If your message doesn't come through to you, just keep trying. Repeat it over and over; never give up, because you could be blocking the message from coming through to you without your even realizing it. Trying it for a while with nothing coming through to you, just ask God for help to open your mind to hear his words coming through to you but also so that you may learn what your body is trying to tell you.

Sometimes, your body doesn't talk with you through words that you hear in your mind; it comes through different feelings you have. All you need to do is to become aware of what your body is telling you, whether it is thoughts in your mind, and/or feelings that you may have.

If you have ever been somewhere, and all of a sudden you had a funny feeling that you should leave immediately, that is a combination of your inner voice and your body telling you that where you are at that particular moment is not very good; so in your best interest just leave. Don't ever question those feelings, just leave.

CHAPER SIX

REMEMBER TO ALWAYS THINK POSITIVE

This is really very simple to understand, but it takes practice to make it happen. The key is to be diligent about the way you think.

It really doesn't matter what you are thinking about, it could be something as simple as someone you know having a real bad cold, and you were in contact with this person, so immediately you start thinking that you are going to catch this bad cold. You are thinking of what to do so that you prevent yourself from getting it, but; in actuality what you are doing is attracting it to you. Your thoughts are of you getting the bad cold and that is what the universe will deliver to you.

If you were with a person who had a bad cold, and when you left him or her you just hoped and prayed that they feel better and dismiss it from your mind, there is a very good possibility that you wouldn't get the cold at all.

Your mind was not attracting the cold to you; so therefore, you won't get it.

This way of thinking is the same and responds the same way in any circumstance.

You have to start re-thinking the way you normally thought. It will be hard at first, because change is always hard at first, but you can always ask God for help. When you ask for help you will see that it is much easier and it will be done for you automatically, sometimes without your even realizing that it happened until later in the day.

If you are thinking negative and that something is going to go wrong, well guess what, IT WILL!!! The exact thing or situation that you were thinking about, will become reality; however, if you asked God you will find that your thoughts will shift to becoming positive and that nothing is going to go wrong.

Don't mistake this for the challenges that God puts in our path, as these are lessons that we need to learn in order to grow; there is a big difference.

I always took a negative situation and turned it into a positive situation, but even I had thoughts that were negative, I am only human. I tried very hard, especially when I was going through challenges, to stay positive. Once I asked God to help me to stay positive and to turn any negative thoughts of mine into positive thoughts, I found myself thinking positive about every situation or challenge that came along.

In the beginning it is hard to think that a simple thing like changing the way you are thinking can change the outcome which you will receive; but that is exactly what happens.

Be patient with yourself and you too will find yourself thinking positive no matter what situation you are in. Most importantly don't forget to ask God for his help.

Anything which you are thinking is exactly what you are going to attract to you, whether you want it or not. There is no way that the Universe will send you the opposite of what you are thinking about, it defies the universe. For no other reason than that, remember to always think positive.

Thinking positive and feeling like whatever you want you already have is very simple once you start applying into your daily life and the rewards of what you attract into your life will totally amaze you!

Your thoughts that you are sending out to the universe, doesn't realize that it is your dream or it is reality, all the energy that you put into these thoughts, will eventually come back to you.

The more energy and you thinking about something, the stronger the energy will go into the universe and return back to you. This is not something that returns to you immediately, there is always a time frame where you change always change your mind on something, otherwise if this were not possible, we would end up fixing all the mistakes in which we were thinking about.

THIS IS SO IMPORTANT TO REMEMBER, AS IT AFFECTS YOUR LIFE IN SO MANY WAYS!

Be persistent in keeping your thoughts positive and soon you will start to see the results.

The outcome might not be what you expected them to be, but you must remember that God knows what is best for us, much better than we do!

It is very hard to realize that a simple thought could change the way the Universe was going to have the energy come to you, but it is very true and should not be taken lightly.

If you seriously want to change your life, you must remember to always think positive and feel that you already have what you want.

I mentioned in Chapter 3 regarding Challenges how always thinking positive works also, but it is such an important message to remember, and how it changes your life is why I wrote a chapter about the effects of thinking positive and having it, enjoying it or the accomplishment of something is very powerful, which the Universe always sends back to us the energy in our thoughts that which we are sending out to the Universe.

CHAPTER SEVEN

LEARN HOW TO RELEASE YOUR DOUBTS, FEARS, ANXIETY, NEGATIVITY AND ANYTHING THAT DOESN'T BELONG IN YOUR BODY OR YOUR MIND TO GOD

All of us have some doubt, fear, negativity and even anxiety in us, even though we might not realize it.

By not releasing this to God, what tends to happen is that these feelings just keep growing inside of us, until our body lets us know one way or the other.

There are many different ways to accomplish this, but I will give you only two ways.

One way, is if someone hurts us and we are feeling the pain, ask God to please take this feeling away, to bless the person who hurt you and also to send that person positive, loving energy. After you ask God to do this, then also ask him to replace what he took from you with whatever you would like, you could leave it up to God's discretion or for instance, you could ask him to replace it with calm, loving, peaceful, faithful, etc energy.

When you remove something negative from your body or mind, you must always replace it with something positive; otherwise, there will be a void and the negativity will creep back in the empty void that is left.

The other way, is ask the angels to bring you a pink basket or bucket and to take all your pain, worry, fears, doubts, anxiety, stress, negativity and anything else that is in your total body also with the situation you are in now; please put them in the pink basket or bucket and bring it to God in heaven to resolve for you. Then you must ask them to replace it with positive, loving, caring, faithful and any other energy God knows that you need. If you desire, you can continue to ask for the energy yourself as to what you would like it replaced with. Remember, always say, "Thank You!"

I prefer doing the second one; every night before going to sleep, along with the rest of my prayers. Personally, I noticed a big difference in my whole being. During some days in which things are hectic, you automatically get anxiety which is very normal; especially in the times in which we are living now. By my doing this prayer, I find myself not having these symptoms as strong as I did prior to my starting this prayer.

God works in strange but miraculous ways! Whatever happens, we might not understand it at the time, or sometimes it might take a couple of months, or even longer.

What happens in our lives could be considered a coincidence, but when you are praying to God and have the faith and trust that he will get you through anything, you will know deep in your heart and soul, that what you experienced was not a coincidence, it was one of God's miracles which he performed just for you.

CHAPTER EIGHT

LISTEN TO YOUR BODY

This is really not as hard as it sounds, matter of fact it is fairly easy to do, once you learn the process. Eventually, you will find yourself automatically listening to your body and what it is telling you without your even realizing it.

To start doing this, you must go back to the quiet place that you decided on, and light your candle.

Look at the candle and just concentrate on your breathing, let your mind empty and become free from any thoughts. Once you have accomplished this, start to concentrate on your body; starting at the top of your head.

Ask your head if there is anything that you should know. Sit there and be patient, listen to see if you are receiving any thoughts in your mind. If you are, remember them, as this is important! Your conscious and/or your sub-conscious mind; or both, are trying to tell you something.

If you have questions, as to what your thoughts mean, just ask. Always be patient and you will receive the answer, never try to rush.

Remember, you have to remain calm and relaxed in order for this process to work.

Keep repeating this process, all the way down to your toes.

If you are getting to many thoughts as you are going through your body, it is fine to stop and repeat the process at some other time.

It is more important that you receive the messages that your body is trying to communicate with you, than trying to hurry through this process.

As you are doing this, you might even feel a sensation, for instance, if you are at your heart, and you ask your heart what message do you have to tell me; you might feel a warm sensation or a feeling that you can't explain, logically thinking, but you know that it means something. Stick with this feeling and ask your heart, "What is this strange feeling, I don't understand why I'm feeling this sensation."

An example of what happened to me just yesterday; here in the Northeast the leaves are falling or most of them have already fallen. Now comes the fun part, raking and bagging them. Well, I have been raking and bagging for 3 days, doing only 7 bags a day and I was tired of looking at the leaves. I asked a friend of mine if they would bring my leaves to the recycling center for me and they were more than happy to help.

Here's where the hard part came in, I had approximately another 21 bags to fill in the course of 4 hours. I asked God and his helpers to help me do the raking and bagging which usually doing the 7 bags took me 2-3 hours. I GOT ALL 21 BAGS DONE IN 3 HOURS!!!

I brought them all to the front of the house and thanked God and his angels for helping me. My friend came and we disposed of them.

My body was still feeling fine, so I decided to mow the lawn for the last time this season.

I only went once around the front yard, and I could feel my legs getting weaker and weaker. I prayed to God and his helpers, to please carry me and just let me push the lawnmower so that I could finish the front and back yard.

Mowing the front and back usually takes me about 1 to 2 hours.

After praying, it literally felt like someone was carrying me, and all I was doing was pushing the lawnmower. I mowed both the front and back in ½ hour.

My legs were not weak at all, they felt great. I thanked God and his helpers again for helping me.

Here is another example of how listening to your body can help you tremendously.

I woke up one morning feeling a very strange weird sensation. When I needed to think about things for some reason I was always drawn to a nearby reservoir. I would always feel better after the visit. I don't know if it was because I would look at the clouds (if they were out) the trees, but mostly I was attracted to the wildlife. The swans always gave me a kind of peacefulness inside because when I watched them, my thoughts immediately went to something that was not only created by God but he/or she was elegant and had a very majestic look to them, whether they were gliding along the water or just staying in place. I also looked at the geese and ducks, but it didn't have the same affect on me. Usually after my visit as I mentioned before I also felt better and then would drive back home, but I knew this time was different as it didn't work.

I felt a very weird sensation, but I couldn't put my finger on why. I spoke with Fran about it, and she told me that I had to go into my body and ask questions, like what is the feeling, is it fear, afraid, etc. Once I got that answer, keep asking questions, until you finally realize why I was feeling this weird feeling.

I went back to the reservoir a couple of days later and just parked there without getting out of my car and continued to watch the swans, so that I could concentrate on what my body was trying to tell me. This is where your ego, plays a very big part in your thinking, so you have to just concentrate on your sensation that you're feeling and where it is in your body, and start asking questions.

When I did this, I heard afraid and scared. I then asked afraid and scared of what? All of a sudden, I sensed and realized what my body was telling me.

At the time, I knew I was loosing my house only didn't know when. It was this part of loosing my house, which was my security for many years, and the fear and being afraid is normal; but you have to let it out of your body and not try to keep it inside. I'm not saying it's easy to do but something that you should do.

As amazing as this sounds . . . All of a sudden a pair of swans; who were on the other side of the reservoir, flew by me 3 times and then landed back on the other side. Each one then lifted a wing, as if to wave to me. That was my confirmation to me, that I heard what my body was trying to tell me.

I thanked my body, and the swans, and then left.

The next day, I didn't go up, but did the following day, and the weird feeling that I was feeling for sometime, was not there.

To me, that was another confirmation; of what my body was trying to tell me. I continue going up there, and no longer have the weird sensation any longer. I know that I kept the fear and being afraid inside me, while my body was trying so hard to make me realize, that it is alright and understand the circumstances to feel this way, but everything will work out fine, because I received such a calm, peaceful, knowingness that somehow everything would work out even better for me than where I am now.

Last night when I said My Appreciation Prayer, I included all the things that they did for me.

When I say My Appreciation Prayer, I thank God for the miracles he did for me that day, the ones I saw and the ones I didn't see. I also tell him everything I appreciate in my life, including my dreams becoming reality, for him helping me to keep my arms open to the abundance he is pouring into my life, keeping my mind open to hear when either him or his helpers are talking with me, and for the miracles he is doing for me for the present and the future, and other things. Then I thank God.

You can include anything you want in this prayer that you want to, but always make sure that you thank God at the end.

CHAPER NINE

BEING ALONE WITH NOBODY NEAR YOU EXCEPT GOD AND HIS HELPERS

Some people, can live alone or with a pet and go to work, come home, go out with friends and be totally happy; but the majority likes someone with whom they can share their experiences, their feelings and most inner thoughts—along with the fact that someone will be there everyday when they get home.

I am not making light of the fact, that there are a lot of singles in society who are wishing for that special someone to come into their life. That's why there are so many online dating sites.

People can become obsessed with the idea of being alone and if they find someone, they automatically think, yes-this is it. There is more to it than that. For those people who think like this, please try to re-think or re-program your mind. If you are looking for someone to spend the rest of your life with, there has to be chemistry between both of you, as well as, having things in common.

If all you want is a one night stand—guess what, in the long run you are still that same lonely person inside; but that's your choice.

Before you start looking for someone to be part of your life, you must first look in the mirror seriously and ask yourself, "What do I see and how do I feel?" If you are not feeling good about yourself and/or if you feel unhappy-then how do you ever expect to attract someone into your life who will make you happy and loved. Remember, always to stay positive and honest with yourself as to what you want in your partner.

We have to feel good about who we are; know what and who we are and decide on what we want. Some might do this very quickly, others it might take time, and still other people might not want to accept this fact and it will take them longer.

Start making of a list of all your good qualities and keep repeating them to yourself. Your list may start out small and everyday when you repeat the words to yourself you will find yourself adding to your list.

Here is an example: As you are starting, you might think of yourself as being a thoughtful, loving, caring, faithful, giving, honest person. That's a great start, but don't stop there. Say these words to yourself, but also let your mind expand and also look inside of yourself, as to the true you.

You will find yourself adding so many things to your list, it will amaze you. Another suggestion, is you can always pray to God and ask him for help to give you help—you will hear the answer as he will say the words in such a loving way, that you will know automatically they came from God, and when you think about the words of describing you, you will realize—Yeah, that's right, how could I have forgotten that. Well add it to your list.

Do this list for as long as necessary, for some of you it might go quickly, for others just take your time, you will know when you're ready.

Once you finally believe in the list that you made or even had God help you make, you start feeling and knowing yourself better and who you really are deep down inside. We all know that people can act one way on the outside, but when you finally get to know this person—guess what—totally opposite.

This is why I am suggesting that you make your list and find out who you really are inside. Then and only then can you start with the next step in the process of being alone and if you want to be with someone.

This next step is the lessons you learnt through your life, and also now that you know yourself-you will know what you will accept and what you won't allow and won't accept under any circumstances with your new partner, if you so decide to find one. This is for you to decide on your own, as everyone is an individual and has his or her own standards to live by.

When meeting a person either face to face, or online; after communicating with them for a while, trust your inner instincts as to whether this person is right for you. Your body will let you know, if you listen and stay in touch with the feelings your body is trying to tell you.

If for example, after communicating with this person, you start to feel a tenseness in your stomach area, chances are your body is trying to tell you something is wrong and what you are looking for in another person is not this one. You might also feel this, as you are emailing each other and see the name come up, or you are on IM and see the other person just got online to chat with you.

On the other hand, if you are finding that when you see an email or IM from this person, you have a very calm, peaceful, happy feeling in your heart area, chances are that you two might be a good match, but again, listen and feel your entire body—not just one part of it.

Being alone with only God and his helpers around is the best feeling ever. It might sound strange for those of you who have not tried it.

When I am feeling lonely, not knowing which way to turn next, this is what I do. I light my candle and start praying to God, usually I am crying and praying at the same time, but as long as you keep your mind open to receiving God's or his helpers messages, they will come to you, by thoughts in your mind. You will know that these are messages from God because they are always in a calm, loving, positive thought and also you will immediately stop crying if you are, and feel like God and all his helpers are all around you.

Ask God, "Please help me, I really don't know what the next step is that I should take in my life? What is going to happen to me?" What you hear back is so soothing, you become totally relaxed, and at the same time you will feel like you can conquer anything that comes your way.

The reason that I left the messages that I receive from God and his helpers out of this book, is because everyone's message is probably different-depending on their individual circumstances; and I would not want to influence you in any way possible of my messages that I receive to your thinking (though your ego might try taking over) that you will receive the same message.

All you have to do is to keep your mind open which is very important and to pray and ask God the questions you would like to have answered by him. Be patient and you will hear God's voice talking with you.

Even though you have heard what God told you, you still have a choice to either listen or to do what you want. God will never hold it against you, if you choose not to listen to his advice. He is very loving and a very forgiving God. He will always love you no matter what.

Once I finished doing this, I don't feel alone anymore. To me, I feel that I am surrounded by God and all his helpers. I don't feel like I am alone anymore, as I feel God and his helpers all around me.

You also can have this feeling, but in order to have this, you have to learn to open your mind to hear what God is telling you. Once you have done this, you too will never be alone again.

Society is becoming more and more aware of the spiritual side of the universe and the effects that it has on humans. It is becoming a very important part of one's life, if they are willing to accept it and believe, have faith and hope. God is the one that creates miracles and no one else.

Also become aware of things around you more, it could be something as simple as a butterfly, flying close by to you; it could even be a bird or flower scent that you suddenly smell when that flower is nowhere to be found. These are some signs that the angels are around you.

CHAPTER TEN

LOOSING YOUR JOB OR BUSINESS

If you or someone you know have lost their job, it can be a very devastating situation.

At first, the individual feels anxiety, stress, hurt, angry and guilt. Normally, the first question that comes to mind is "Why Me?" what did I do wrong.

Unfortunately, this is how the world has become. The bigger the corporation or business, the less concerned they are with the employees. All they are looking for is to keep their profits up so they can have the top executives keep living the lifestyle that they have become accustomed to, and not even give a thought to the affect it has on an employee.

There are a lot of businesses, closing down in one location, leaving everyone to loosing their job and moving to another location, where they hire employees for less money and therefore their own profits increase.

I guess you call this democracy, but personally, I think it is totally wrong and somehow should be stopped.

I don't want to get into the political field either, but shipping our jobs in the U.S. overseas and leaving our country with our people on unemployment or loosing their business that they have built from the ground up and not being able to compete with the so-called "Big Boys" is a total shame.

These small companies are so personal and treat a customer like an individual and not just a number. This is how the United States started to grow and personally I think this is how we need to get back to the grass roots. Small companies create jobs, but they also have a very nice relationship with their employees (granted there are a few that think like the larger companies—but most don't) and these small companies are concerned about their employees and I am not going to deny that they want to make a profit also. That's why they went into business to begin with, but making a profit with concern for their employees is a totally different aspect than having a large corporation make a profit and keep it amongst the upper echelon and lay employees off and the ones that are left, now have to work twice as hard to complete the work which needs to be done. The other option, which bigger companies take, is ship it overseas—have the work done there, and then they ship it back. Bingo—our U.S. jobs are depleted!!!

When I lost my business, even though I did believe in God, I kept beating myself up mentally. Besides trusting people whom (I was so naïve) I thought everyone was just like I was—very trustworthy. I didn't learn the lesson the first or second time, so it came back again. This time with such force, that it forced me to go out of business.

I felt sorry for my employees, even though I was a small business, it didn't matter; but I also felt sorry for my customers. It was like I let them down someway.

It would keep going over and over in my mind, what could I do, so that I may start my business all over again. I prayed, cried, prayed and kept hearing, "You did everything that you could under the circumstances, except learn your lesson the first time around of not trusting everyone."

Honestly, hearing that did not console me, but I did understand. It took me about 6 months before I totally understood the whole picture behind the business.

During that time, sure I had friends to talk to which I am grateful for, but I didn't get that peacefulness until I lit my candle and talked to God. Once I finally understood the whole picture, there was so much more involved than my just being trustworthy which forced me out of business. There were outside forces which were acting against me, unbeknown to me at the time, to make it successful, despite everything I tried.

There were many, many challenges which I went through and God helped me through all of them as I had mentioned in my previous chapter.

One important thing which happened in my life during this time was that I finally had the chance to become closer to God and learnt how to become closer to the spiritual world; which I am totally grateful for.

While working, like we all do, there is not enough time in the day to do what we want to accomplish, much less to learn how to become closer to the spiritual world. Some of us might have taken out time in our lives to do it, but I to have admit, even though I believed in God and prayed, while working, it is totally different for me now. I also feel as every day passes that I am becoming even closer and more aware of my surroundings and enjoying every single one of them. It could be something as simple as watching a bird eat or just land on a branch of a tree. I notice the beauty of the bird and also realize despite what they have to do to survive, most of them do—it is God's gift to us for us to enjoy their beauty.

It doesn't have to cost money, just to walk outside and enjoy nature or go for a walk, look up into the sky and watch the clouds if it's during the day, and if it's at night look at the stars. Once you start realizing the beauty that is all around you, you start to appreciate every single thing you have, including your own well being as well as other things that God has created.

Also one most important thing has happened to me, being laid off and loosing the business.

I became closer to God and his helpers, and I am becoming more and more spiritual as every day passes.

This definitely would not have happened if I stayed on the path I was on; so I am truly grateful for that.

Another important aspect of my life which happened because of my personal situation was that I was able to write this book, to help others get through the same or very similar situations. I thank God for that all the time, if I could just change one person's life, then all the effort I put into writing this book was well worth it and I'm glad. If I can help more, then I would be ecstatic!

CHAPTER ELEVEN

FACING UNEMPLOYMENT AND/OR FORECLOSURE ON YOUR HOME

I am not going to tell you that this is easy, because this is a very hard thing for most people. Granted to some people, it doesn't bother, but I truly believe the majority of people have many different feelings about the situation they are in.

We will talk about unemployment first. There are feelings of being scared, angry, hurt, humility, etc. One of the first things that comes to mind is how am I going to pay my bills. No matter how much you try to cut back, your unemployment check is not going to make ends meet.

You have pride and really don't want to ask for help, as you have always supported yourself or your family constantly and now you are facing this.

As far as foreclosure on your home, by far I think that this is the biggest test of our faith. First of all, you have to leave your home that you worked so hard for all these years and it is not by choice, it is because of lack of money to be able to support the mortgage.

The fortunate ones are the people who fall under the government's program, but what about the rest of us—we are left so to speak out in the cold.

If our credit is good and we have enough income, then we can still find someplace to stay, but those whose credit was ruined because they couldn't afford to keep up the payments, with the high interest rates being charged at one time—where do these people go to live. Besides if they have animals, most places don't accept animals, so therefore they not only lost their job, home but have to make another hard decision as to what to do with their pet(s).

For those of you who are pet lovers, you will understand this, for those of you who aren't, this will probably not make sense and your comment to someone in this predicament might be something to the effect, just give them away. For those of us who are pet lovers, they are just like part of the family. These people end up with 3 challenges; loosing our job or business and being on unemployment, their credit ruined because of not being able to pay and lastly to loose their home.

They do have agencies which help, but one must first have to realize that pride does not pay the bills which need to be paid, and also you have to eat. If you own an animal, they have to eat too and be taken care of. They were always there for you while you were working, and believe me when I say this, they sense the tension that you are going through, but somehow they just give you their unconditional love, which in turn gives you the strength to do whatever you have to, in order to get help.

Again, I turned to God and asked for his help. I heard an inner voice say call, so I said OK call who and heard look in the phone book.

As strange as this may sound, but its the absolute truth, as I randomly opened the phone book—it was to the page I needed. I called the number and got immediate help. I thanked the person on the other end and then I thanked God for his assistance in helping me so quickly.

That was the hardest thing I ever had to do, or so I thought at the time, I felt so humiliated in doing it, I just started to cry while being interviewed and I remember telling the lady, if you told me I would be in this position 5 years ago, I would have told you no way. She was just like an angel, she replied to me, you're not alone, there are a lot of people in your situation now with the situation this country is in—who never thought they would be like you either, it is nothing to feel ashamed about, just Thank God that this program is available to help people.

This woman at the agency, who interviewed me, said that I should also apply for other things, because of my low income I would qualify. That was a little to much for me to handle at the moment, but I took the paperwork that she offered to me and thanked her for everything.

When I came home, I lit my candle, started crying because I had to ask for help and I felt so humiliated. I prayed and thanked God for helping me through this agency, but even though I needed it, I prayed that by giving it to me, that it didn't mean that someone who needed it more than me would be denied. Almost immediately, I stopped crying and heard that everyone that needs help, will get the help, they just have to meet the qualifications and everything will be fine. It felt like God and all his helpers were all around me, and I was at such peacefulness so suddenly, I knew that it was God and his helpers.

I was very fortunate to have people whom I contacted about my situation and they were willing to accept $10.00 per week from my check. These were people that I never met, but they were so nice and understanding of what was happening with people loosing their jobs. I'm not talking about friends, I mean like the electric, water, insurance company. This is unheard of, but I was very fortunate and blessed to meet these people. The only company that would not work with me was the phone company, if I couldn't pay the bill in full when it came due, they would shut me off, very simple for them and also the mortgage and credit card companies—they wanted their monthly amount due and paid then and had no remorse at all, even when I explained my situation and could only pay a partial payment. They didn't want the partial payment; they wanted the whole thing which was due for the month. My reply to them was I hope you never get in the predicament that I'm in as well as many other people, because you would never survive. I was probably wrong in saying that and should have been more understanding that they were just doing their job, but if all the rest of these people whom I was dealing with could understand—what was their problem.

I am at the time of writing this book, in the situation of all three things; loosing my business, job and now loosing my home with no place to go, because my credit score is no longer good, with the loss of income and I also have cats. I treat my cats, like most animals lovers, treat them as if they are part of your family.

The only thing which is getting me through this is, first of all God, his angels and helpers, and sending me through other people to give me additional support in any way possible. By no means am I saying it is easy!

This is a very hard and challenging situation, and yes I cried many a night wondering what I could do to change my situation—but the easy answer was to find a job, the reality of that is there aren't very many jobs out there.

Packing my things to move to someplace unknown at this point is painful and yes scared of the unknown.

The only peace and what gives me the strength to go on is that I know God has a different path for me to be on, which is much better and happier than the path I was on.

Even though we might not think that it's right to have to go through all the pain, hurt, anguish, humility, challenges, etc., it does teach us lessons in life in which we must learn to grow and in turn we become more spiritual.

God is always waiting for us, it is we who have to ask for help, and help will arrive. It might not be as expected, but we can never forget the fact that God always knows what is best for us and that he wants us to live our lives in happiness and not in despair.

My advice to all of you who read this book, is pray to God, you will start to see results, but you must remain positive and with an open mind. With God, his angels and helpers by your side; you can survive anything! You will also be able to remain calm and peaceful, knowing that there is a better life ahead for you and your outlook on life will be totally amazingly different, somehow, someway you know that you are being led down a path which God knows that first of all, you will be happy, but also one that will bring you a sense of peace and tranquility.

CHAPTER TWELVE

Replace Your Anger And Hurt

All of us either get hurt or angry at a loved one, relative, friend, co-worker and even a stranger. It could be a lot of ways that our feelings are hurt or we get angry.

One way is that we think that we should be getting more attention, or something that was said to you that hurt you and made you angry. As far as a co-worker or boss, it might be that we think we should receive more recognition for the work which we performed and/or the criticism which we get for our work that we know is right and not wrong as they are saying. Also a stranger might say something to you that you didn't deserve to hear, for instance, you are pulling into a parking spot as you were there first and when you get out of the car you see this person behind your vehicle, yelling at you that you took their place—while all the time they were nowhere in site. It could be anything that someone says or does, even doesn't do, that would make you angry or hurt.

If you are a sensitive person, you will feel this even more so than the average person. You are the kind of person who really has to be aware of what happened, how you feel and learn to release the hurt or anger, just as important as for everyone else, but with you being so sensitive, you will sense it quicker.

Holding the anger and hurt in does not do anything to the individual who actually hurt you or made you angry it only hurts your body. The longer that you hold this in the more damage is does to your body without your even realizing it, until something happens to you and you get sick. You still might not even realize that the reason you got sick is because of the anger and hurt you have been carrying around inside you for so long. Most likely, you will just accept the fact that you got sick and then start concentrating on getting better.

By doing this you are not alone, there are many people who don't even realize how much anger and hurt they are carrying around in their own body caused by someone else. You must release this anger and hurt so that your body can heal and remember to do this every time you get angry or hurt.

This is not a complicated task to perform. All you have to do is to sit quietly somewhere where you will not be disturbed and empty your mind of everything that you're thinking of and just relax.

Once in this relaxed state, pray to God and ask him to take away all the pain, the anger and hurt which was caused by—and you can start naming the names of the people who hurt you and at the end of your list also include and all the rest of the people.

After you have asked God to do this, also remember to ask them to Bless Them and to put his Divine Love Light around them with positive, loving energy.

Now that you removed something from your body, this means that there is a void in the area where you were harboring all this hurt, pain and anger so you must replace it with something otherwise negative energy fills in the void very quickly, so you ask God to please replace what he took away from you with positive, loving, faithful, honest, caring and any other energy that he knows is best for you.

Most importantly after you do this, do not ever forget to Thank God for all of his help.

Now that God removed all of the anger, pain and hurt you will feel much better; but you have to constantly remember to do this whenever you are angry, hurt or in pain that someone did to you either on purpose or unintentionally.

By praying to God for help to release this from your body and Bless the person or persons who did it to you and also by sending them positive, loving energy and also have God replace what he took from you and with whatever energy you ask him to do for you and also what he knows you need, you will be totally amazed at the difference you will feel in your body.

From my own personal experience, I held so much hurt, pain and anger in me for so many years, I never realized it, just like I mentioned before that you probably wouldn't—which is fine and normal. We just go on with our everyday life and don't think about it.

Well for me, I ended up getting sick. I knew I would get better and prayed to God and also Archangel Raphael to do a healing on me.

I had a business card for Fran DeSeno, to whom I dedicated this book to, but didn't know where I put it. I wasn't going to keep her card but something told me to, so I did.

Some people would rather take medication prescribed by their doctor with a very good possibility they could cause another problem either at the start or down the road if they continually take them. Everybody has to make their own decision but as for me, if I can heal the natural way—that's the way I'm going to do it.

Well, I prayed to God to please help me and all of a sudden Fran's card showed up on the kitchen table. So I figured, I have nothing to loose and everything to gain—it's natural and the energy healing comes from God, so I called her and made an appointment with her.

She talked with me for some time before she started doing the healing on me, what she had found out is that all my pain, hurt and anger had built up around my heart, and that when I was stressed or had anxiety that is when it would flair up.

Fran, also taught me so much, not only how to perform Reiki on myself and others (as I went to the classes) but also brought me closer to God and taught me how to get back my self confidence and everything else that I had lost by letting other's control me instead of my controlling my own feelings.

There was this man that Fran knew who was having a class on "Healing with Horses" and Fran said to me that we should go together. So I went, there were 4 horses and I was originally drawn to this black horse before the class started and asked him if he could heal my heart for me. He took his nose and went from my heart to my stomach about 5-10 minutes, even though other people were walking by, he never stopped. Then he did, I thanked him" and went to say hello to the other horses. By then the class was ready to start.

Well to my surprise, the horse that was to do the healing was this black horse that I was talking with. We went through a meditation procedure first and then the man having this class, had me come into the pen area and I noticed another horse but there was a gate between the black horse and the beige colored horse. He told me to stand approximately six feet away and put my hands down to my side with my palms facing the horse. He then asked me if I felt anything, I said yes it feels like someone is pushing against my hands. He asked me if he could share it with the rest of the class and I said sure, which he did. Then he told me to take 3 steps closer to the horse and stop and stay in the same position. I did that also and he asked me now what do you feel, I said, "Oh, My God, I feel this very strong, peaceful energy not only in my hands but across my whole chest area. He also shared this with the rest of the class, then told me to walk up to the horse and pet his neck which I did gladly. The horse to my amazement did the same thing as when he was in the stable, he took his nose and went from my heart to my stomach about 3 or 4 times. I gave the horse a kiss and said Thank you as my time was up. I left the pen area for the next person to go in and I noticed the black horse went over to the beige horse and I got the impression that they were talking, at least that's what entered my mind.

He went through the rest of the class, and then brought us all in the barn and said whoever could put the leas around the 4 horses first would win a free class with him, well I did. This beige horse was on the other side of the stable and looking out the window and I asked him to please come over to me, the horse turned his head to look at me, made that muzzle sound and came over to me. To my amazement, despite the rest of the class in the barn, he did the same thing as the black horse. He went from my heart to my stomach for about 25-30 minutes and I immediately felt cured. I thanked him and gave him a kiss between his nose and eyes.

Fran continues doing her healings on me, but not as frequently as I needed in the beginning.

God and his helpers are also helping me by my openness to listen to them and hear what they have to say.

I have had so many challenges, as I'm sure some or most of you have had, but I also learnt so many lessons and took the responsibility of the situation I was in.

God and his helpers not only helped me through everything, but I became closer to God and all his helpers, a stronger person, and I always helped anyone that I could, but now I can do this with a knowing that God is guiding me and I am working through him to help whoever needs help.

It might be as simple as just saying the words that a particular person needed to hear at that time. I hear that from strangers that I meet at a nearby reservoir where I make sure the wildlife are fine and not hurt, clean the area of fishing line, hooks, etc and also talk to the people that are there.

More than once, they say to me, something told me to come here, I didn't know why, but I came and I needed to hear what you just said to me, Thank you very much. I don't even remember what I said, that's how I know it came directly through me from God to pass on to them to hear. It is such a nice feeling.

CONCLUSION

I started packing and giving things away still not knowing where I was going to live, at this time I figured I would be living in my car with my cats.

When someone would ask me how did I expect to do that and where would I go, I just said I have no idea but there is no way that I'm giving up my cats and somehow someway everything will be alright.

As usual, God opened doors for me that I hadn't even thought about, which I am very grateful.

Where I'm living now is a very nice area. I have a spacious, lovely place to live, but most importantly I was able to bring my cats with me.

I have met people that I would have never have met before had I not been forced to move, but more importantly—some of these strangers opened up their hearts to me and they treat me like family. Everyone that I have met, I usually smile and say "Hello" and this is the first time that I can remember that the smile and

Hello is returned to me with the same sincerity as I said it to them. It is such a great feeling.

Now in the mornings, I go outside to have my cup of coffee to welcome in the new day and the surroundings around me and enjoy it and look forward to every new second of each day with love and passion because I know something will happen that God has put in my sight or I will hear by my inner voice telling me.

Yes, I am not saying loosing everything was easy—it was very hard but I learnt many lessons and you have to go on and look toward a future filled with love, promise and harmony and appreciate everything and everyone around you. I always took a negative and turned it into a positive-that's just part of who I am but now thanks to God and his helpers I am so much more fulfilled with the knowledge and difference I can make. If you can look at every day the way I do now, you will be blessed by God also, just like I am.

God also opened the door for the possibility of this book getting published which I am very grateful for.

If you enjoyed reading this book, watch for my next book "Amazing Wildlife-My True Life Experiences."

I have God and his helpers to thank for that also, he has helped me in so many, many ways and still is that I have only given you a few examples in comparison as to what he has given me.

ABOUT THE AUTHOR

I was always close to my father. Despite him working sometimes long hours, he would always find time or an opportunity to bring me some place with him when he was doing an odd job for someone. He was always trying to teach me things about life or explain to me what he was doing and why. Also when he had free time, we would take a walk in the woods to see the nature, he would tell me the different birds that we saw and the sounds they made, or a tree and what kind it was, in what stage of growth it was in and the purpose for the tree.

One day he said to me he has a surprise to show me but wouldn't tell me what it was. Being young I was really excited. When we arrived at his friends farm, that's when he told me what had happened. His friend was mowing his hayfield and didn't see a doe laying down and accidentally hurt him with the mower. Thankfully it wasn't hurt bad, but he immediately stopped the tractor, picked up the doe and ran back to the farm, fixed his leg and was nursing him back to health. My father knowing how much I loved and cared for animals and never seeing a deer much less a doe, he thought it would be nice for me to see. I was sad that it had gotten hurt despite it being an accident but when I saw the doe, my eyes opened with amazement---YOU WOULD NEVER KNOW THIS DOE WAS HURT! He was standing there just looking at us as we entered the barn and came to his stall, munching on the grass as if that was such a normal every day occurrence and its where he should have been. I fell in love with him immediately. My father told me the following week, the doe was so healthy that his friend let it go but the doe always sticks around waiting for him to come into the field, like he was saying hello and then would scamper off into the woods.

I have always enjoyed helping people, whether it be just talking or otherwise. As I said before, I always loved and cared for animals. Somehow, people started showing up at my door, even strangers besides neighbors, asking me if I have seen their cat or dog, (they probably saw me feeding the strays that came to me or were sent to me by other means. I would say No if I hadn't and then ask for the pet's name and a description. I would also ask for their name and phone number. We agreed to exchange this information to keep each other informed.

I told them to give their pet 3 days to come home. Usually during that time frame, their pet showed up at my door and I called them to re-unite them--it is always such a great feeling. Sometimes, but not often, they don't show up by the 3rd afternoon so I just sit, clear my mind, and picture what the pet looks like and call their name. I tell them that they have to go home because they are loved and missed very much and they should do it immediately.

The next morning, I always get a call from the pet's owner telling me their pet showed up and then they thanked me. I would always say to them I'm glad I could help but you're thanking the wrong person, you should be thanking God as he is the one who made it possible.

I have helped deer, raccoons, rabbits, squirrels, etc. and now it is being expanded by God to helping wildlife as I tell you in my next book coming out, called, "Amazing Wildlife-My True Life Experiences."

I would appreciate any comments or questions you might have. Please write to me at Aswana.Angels@ yahoo.com.

Also if you are interested in a long distance healing from Fran, please don't hesitate to contact me and I will pass on your name, address, telephone number (best time to call, also with your email address, if possible) with a message to her and she will return your call.